At first glance in NFT Investing for Kids and Beginners

Introduction to Non-Fungible Token: Crypto, Bitcoin, Blockchain, and Stocks Investment for Dummies

Sweet Smart Books

from various sources. Please consult a licensed professional before attempting any techniques outlined in this book.

By reading this document, the reader agrees that under no circumstances is the author responsible for any losses, direct or indirect, that are incurred as a result of the use of the information contained within this document, including, but not limited to, errors, omissions, or inaccuracies.

Table of Contents

Introduction

The world has come with its fair share of surprises, and technology certainly has gone a whole lot further than many of us have even come to realize. With the metaverse, a digital world right on our doorstep, we cannot keep ignoring the opportunities that await us in the decentralized universe.

But even throwing the word decentralized is enough to give an average person a headache. Why is that? Because the world of crypto and NFT seem complicated. With the various terminology, anyone who dives in to try and learn how the basics work is immediately thrown off. It becomes very hard.

But if you are still interested in learning about NFTs, and investing in the world of crypto, then you have come to the right place! This is where I will be taking a simplified but accurate approach to investing in NFTs for both children and beginners. Complex ideas will be explained in easy terms, and you will learn everything you need to get started in this digital world.

Learning about crypto and NFT is a journey, as there is quite a lot of information to cover, and both have an interesting approach to being successful. Does this book guarantee success? Any book that does, you should question its validity. This book is here to help boost your chances of success, aid you in avoiding common mistakes, and give you enough so that you have what it takes to truly become a savvy investor.

Where you no longer have to concern yourself about scouring the web left, right, and center, this book will provide you with all the necessary resources and where else you can look to learn more. You will learn where you can practice investing, as well as learn everything about NFTs.

Soon you will realize how simple and easy cryptocurrency and NFTs are, and that the only difference with it is how it is being explained. You won't have to worry about confusion and see that there is even a place for you in the investment world. The future waits for no one, and it is up to us to catch up.

So, catch your ride on this train. As we break down everything you need to know so that by the time you step off, you will have the confidence to take the next step forward in the world of decentralized finances, where the terminology will no longer even scare you!

Chapter 1: Understanding Investing

To understand how to make money with NFTs and with crypto, let's break down the first action: investing. What exactly is investing, and what can it do for you? I don't think anyone can stress enough the importance of investing in the world and the sad reality that more people can better their lives if they believe themselves capable of investing.

Investing Explained

Investing is specifically defined as placing a resource, normally money, into something that is expected to give a profit or income. You can invest in all sorts of things, such as businesses, assets, houses, or even NFTs and cryptocurrency.

Investing involves a level of risk and return. What does this mean? It means that although you are putting your money into something, it does not guarantee that you will always be making money from this. Why is this so important? Because both crypto and NFTs are known to be risky investments.

There is a general idea that the greater the risk the greater the reward. So, if you have a bigger chance of losing the money you also have a bigger chance of getting more money.

After all, Bitcoin had turned people into millionaires practically overnight (Bitcoin is the first cryptocurrency). But people cannot ignore the fact that Bitcoin has also gotten people into deep debts and various other issues.

So guaranteed success does not exist within the world of investing. There are boosted chances of success, however. Investing, especially in crypto and NFTs, does require a higher level of strategy and skill.

Pros and Cons of Investing

So, what exactly can you get from deciding to invest? Why should you consider investing in the first place? Is it as important as people are saying?

If people keep telling you to invest but fail to explain why, then I understand why you would hesitate to jump into this. After all, we are born in a generation that focuses more on instant gratification, rather than focusing on the rewards of the future. But those who have adopted the mindset of learning from the past, working in the present, and looking to the future are far more likely to achieve the success that so many people could only dream and hope to achieve.

Investing is one of the few key ways of achieving financial freedom. Depending on your age, it might not be so important to you right now, but you do understand that when you want to live on your own, you've got bills to pay, a job to run, as well as household duties to keep up with.

So When Do People Have Time For Themselves?

That is the scary question. Due to society and the workforce in this day and age, people rarely have time for themselves nor can they afford to. This is where investing comes in.

Investing allows you to build a bigger income so that you can open up your time and be able to afford things in life that you would like to do. This would include traveling or supporting your hobby in art.

Investing allows you to build massive wealth over time. This is a little bit where the catch is involved. Investing, even in crypto, is not going to make you rich overnight. Those who have become rich overnight by investing in NFTs and cryptocurrency are like those who have won the lottery. It is incredibly rare, and it does happen, but it is best not to take your chances on luck and rather focus on strategy.

You do not have to be a mathematical genius or have a degree to invest successfully. All you need to do is spend the necessary time learning how to master the market and analysis skills, as well as get the help of many tools and tricks available for people online.

There are also crypto, NFTs, and regular stocks that can suit whatever you would like and whatever suits your goals. Naturally, you will want a plan, and you can make an investment choice based on what best suits your plan. A good example would be investing in Ethereum if you are interested in investing in the multiverse, or NFTs, considering that the majority of NFTs and multiverse platforms run on Ethereum's blockchain (which will be explained later).

You don't have to be wealthy to start investing. You can start small and gradually build up your funds and capital. It is certainly the preferred choice in comparison to getting yourself a loan or borrowing money you cannot pay back. So, start small, and work with the money that you can afford to lose.

When investing, it helps to beat inflation and grow your overall account. What is inflation? Inflation is the percentage of when prices go up. The price of gas is certainly not what it was ten years ago. If you want to do a fun little project, find out how much a horse cost a hundred years ago in dollars compared to what a horse costs now, and you will see the difference and how inflation has affected all the markets.

However, there is always a downside to investing that you always need to be careful of. Investing for starters can take a lot of time. This means that if you were hoping that investing in NFTs and cryptos might solve your problems right away, unfortunately, this is not always the case. The main factor that plays a role in earning money in investments is time, and the more time you have, the bigger the advantage. So, starting to invest while you are so young is incredibly wise, and your older self will be thanking your younger self for this decision that you have made.

The NFT and crypto markets are incredibly volatile. This means that although the value of coins and NFTs can go up, it can also come crashing down. And you can't always predict the direction in which it goes. That means when it comes to investing, you will always have to keep an eye on your investments. This is not something you can simply buy and leave and forget about. Although there are certainly investment opportunities that work like this, when it comes to crypto and NFTs, you will always have to be monitoring the markets.

You can also lose a whole lot of money if you do not know what you are doing. Walking into investing blindly is like walking around and putting your money into slots not knowing you just put money into a post office box. There are ways that you can so easily lose money if you are not aware or alert. This counts heavily for crypto as well as NFTs. The online world is not as safe as we'd like it to be, so we need to practice caution. Just because we don't always see a threat doesn't mean that it is not there.

Trading Explained

Sometimes trading and investing are used interchangeably, but there is a difference between the two, and the majority of it has to do with the timeline.

When you are investing, it focuses on the long-term, where you buy assets and hold on to them for over a year to even a couple of decades.

When you are trading, it focuses on the short-term, where you buy assets and hold on to them for a couple of hours, days, or even months. Day trading is very common practice with highly volatile investments, such as cryptocurrency, and you might not even be holding on to NFTs that long, depending on your goals and what you are working with.

Trading is a far more hands-on approach, where you will have to be monitoring the markets for much longer and spend time learning about the short-term trends over the long term-trends.

And what are some of the pros and cons of trading?

Crypto and NFT trading are highly accessible for people who want to trade individually. It is an easy and simple process to set up an account, as well as to get started. Considering everything is digital, all trading takes place online, and, unless you are using a broker, can even run 24/7 (unlike the common stocks that have their opening and their closing times).

There is a greater potential for you to receive faster returns in comparison to many other investments. This is naturally because the market moves at a quicker pace and allows you to earn more money than you may have with other forms of investment.

However, the volatility, as much as it can be a bonus, can also be a problem. Volatility can cause a whole lot more losses than what you might receive with less risky investment or trading choices. There is a big reason why this is being drilled in now, because not enough people take the risks seriously enough, which leads to breaking some common trading rules which, in turn, gets you kicked out of the trading game before you barely even started.

Top Rules to Follow When Investing

So when diving into investing, especially as a beginner, there are a couple of rules you need to follow. Many savvy investors follow the same rules, and they all play a role in success. Some investors repeat these rules over and over again because they see how other people are constantly breaking them, without realizing that is exactly what is holding them back. So be sure to come back and revise these rules now and then.

- Understand the power of compounding. This is when you add the investments you receive back into your other investments to earn greater amounts of money. Some accounts already do this for you. Compound interest is one of the best ways to make money work for you, so always see where you can apply matters of compound interest in whatever form of investment you make.
- Do not ever put all your eggs in the same basket. This is especially applicable if you are working with highly volatile investments. You want to spread the risk by buying into different cryptocurrencies and NFTs. As an investor, it might be wise if you even consider other investment avenues other than NFTs and cryptocurrency.

- Avoid credit card debt or taking on a loan when investing. This follows one of the most classic rules: do not use money in an investment that you cannot afford to lose. Your very goal with investing is to be better off than where you are now, so if you get yourself into debt and then lose the money while investing in incredibly risky choices, then you are certainly in a worse place than you would have been if you had simply decided to stick with the money you had. You might have still countered a loss, but you would not have been in trouble.
- Investing doesn't have to be complicated. I feel people make investing a whole lot more difficult than it should be, but in reality, this is far from the truth. The reason why investing can be seen as difficult is over the fact there might just be a lot to remember. But once you have all the facts dished out for you, it is quite easy to work with them.
- Remember that no investor is perfect, so all the choices you make have to be determined by the evidence you see and your logic. Following investor gurus and experts blindly without your research is opening up room for even more mistakes or falling for scams. Many of these investor gurus make money through their education rather than the investment themselves.
- You must focus on investing consistently. Consistency is key when it comes to any kind of skill or trade. Trading is certainly a skill to be

learned, and therefore staying consistent and practicing regularly is important for your overall investment journey.

- It might seem odd, but patience is key. Regardless of whether you are working with volatile investments, having the grit to sit through the lows, or waiting before jumping blindly into an investment everyone is partaking in is a very rare and invaluable skill. Being able to hold back or push through is not as easy when you are busy in the live markets. So, one of the skills you have to learn would be patience.
- Risk is not your biggest enemy. This may seem odd, but many investors are too afraid of portfolio risks. Sure, they focus on staying safe, but in the end, may end up with minimal returns. Now if you are working with NFTs and Crypto, you will anyways start to work with a higher level of risk. This is not the end of the world as some people may be considering; this may be the first type of backlash you may very well be receiving from your peers.
- Only pick cryptocurrency and NFTs that you are comfortable with. You want to focus on topics and digital coins that you are familiar with and fully understand. Because if you lack understanding, you may fail to identify any sorts of indications that crypto or NFT is going to fail, or whether it has the potential to last in the long term.
- Emotions in a market of logic are a person's biggest enemy. So be sure to learn a little bit of

trading psychology, and to focus on good emotional habits to aid in your trading success.

- Be sure that you build up a good investment portfolio and plan your goals before entering the markets. Without a plan, you are planning to fail. So be sure to have your investment plans and goals in writing.
- Timing in the market is not altogether a winning strategy. Although timing certainly does help, it should not be your primary strategy. This is because it is nearly impossible to time your purchases perfectly, especially in a market that focuses on its volatility.
- Always take your time with doing the necessary research, an extra five to ten minutes can sometimes even make you pick out a scam from a legitimate investment. But always understanding what is going on in the news, and the markets.

Many of these rules may seem obvious, until it comes to applying them in the trading world itself. We have just now simply taken a look at trading and investing, and now it is time to take a peek at the topics at hand. Cryptocurrency and NFT have taken the world by storm, and there is so much that still needs to be learned. So staying up to date on NFT and crypto matters is key.

Investing in crypto and investing in NFT do have some big differences, considering their circumstances and how they work. That is why it is best to choose one topic you would like to work and master before moving on to the next. For example, investing in crypto requires more analytical skills, whereas working with NFTs requires more entrepreneurial skills. Therefore, whichever one is your strongest point is naturally the one recommended for you to pursue.

But to work with NFTs, you need to understand the basics of cryptocurrency. This is because NFTs are built on the blockchain of crypto, very specifically Ethereum. That is, although we are mostly focused on NFTs, we're still brushing over the basics of cryptocurrency within this book.

Chapter 2: Understanding Digital Currency

Whenever a lot of people talk about cryptocurrency, the idea of coins being transferred online to and from is probably what comes to mind. And although the idea is not far off, cryptocurrency more works in forms of code, and there is no physical coin that actually exists.

Crypto Understood

Cryptocurrency is a form of digital currency, and it is secured by a form of cryptography. This means that despite the coin being digital, a person cannot make copies or try double-spending it. So, digital coins will work very closely to physical coins, as there are even digital wallets that are involved.

The very first form of cryptocurrency that was designed was Bitcoin, which was launched in 2009 by the pseudonym Satoshi Nakamato. An interesting fact? No one really knows who invented Bitcoin, although people have had their suspicions.

Cryptocurrency purely works online, and it is built in the system called blockchain.

Blockchain Explained

The beauty about blockchain is that you need to understand the basic simplified concept of it in order to be able to work with it, but you do not need to understand every single detail.

Not unless you are planning on creating and designing your very own blockchain, which means you might have just purchased the wrong book.

Here, we are going to explain the simple concepts of blockchain, and why it works so well.

Blockchain works like a digital ledger. That means it records every single transaction that is made. But it is designed in a way that makes it impossible to tamper with the information.

So let's start off with the reason why blockchain exists. Imagine you wanted to buy a beautiful cottage. In this world, everyone who owns a cottage keeps a little ledger booklet.

You find a nice cozy cottage, and you want to see the ledger in order to see the history of the cottage. And in the last four years, the cottage has:

- 2018 - replaced a broken window
- 2019 - exterminate cockroaches
- 2020 - repainted the porch
- 2021 - repaired creaky floors

Now you are getting the ledger, and this is the information you see:

- 2018 - replaced a broken window
- 2019 - chimney cleaned
- 2020 - repainted the porch
- 2021 - repaired creaky floors

You might have noticed that not only was information removed, but information that was put in that did not even happen. What does this tell you? Well, the owner is obviously not being honest about the incidents around the cottage.

How would you fix this problem?

Well, you get an intermediary involved.

But this funny person has a forgetful memory and is sometimes known to accept bribes.

So that defeats the entire purpose.

This is when blockchain steps in. This is a digital system and imagine if each cottage owned a blockchain. And every time a transaction is completed, it is automatically logged into the blockchain.

So, starting with 2018's information, it is placed into the first block called the 'Genesis' block. This information is secured, and a special key is formed. What does this key do? It changes into a totally different design if even one small thing were to change in the information that was provided.

Ok. So, what next?

Well, now the information of 2019 is put in, and this makes a second block. But before the second block's design is made, it contains block one's first key. Then the second key is designed.

So, if information is changed on block one, it changes block one's key. If that happens, then it changes the information on the second block, and the second block's key changes as well.

Then 2020's information forms a third block, and the copy of key one and key two are placed in the third block before the third key is made.

Are you now starting to understand what is happening?

Now, you also have a string of information on this one cottage. But this string, this 'blockchain', also has copies. There are hundreds of copies of this exact same string of information about the cottage. They all are syncing. So, what happens if you change one or two copies of information on the string?

Well, ten to fifteen minutes later, if these two strings do not match up with the rest of the strings of information, then those two strings are reverted back to the original information.

This is one way to describe blockchain. And each string of information is actually a computer that holds a copy of the information.

Glass Box Analogy

One of my favorite analogies of blockchain would also be that of the glass box. Blockchain works like a bank vault. You walk in and see rows and rows of transparent boxes. You can see all the contents inside, but you cannot interact with it.

However, if you own a private and public key (of your crypto coin), then you have both the address of your glass box, and the private key acts as the key to unlock and work with the contents inside the glass box. You do not own the glass box, but you can work with the tokens.

And that is roughly how blockchain works. You want to understand that there is a lot of things running blockchain, but if you understand that:

- The information is transparent, you as the user are anonymous.
- Once you have done a transaction, you will not be able to reverse it.
- Blockchain is very secure and considered as tamper-proof.
- All the information is verified by 'miners' across the globe, so it will be impossible to determine who will be verifying your transaction.
- Public keys act like the address to your account, and private keys give you permission to use the

tokens. So if you lose your private keys, then you won't ever be getting it back.

Mining Described

I will not be going deep into mining. Mining is a necessary part of blockchain, and without miners, blockchain won't work so well as we would like. Basically, miners on blockchain solve complex puzzles. They are then rewarded with the blockchain's tokens. They also verify the transactions through the solving of these puzzles.

It sounds odd, but it works. However, cryptocurrencies using the PoW (Proof of Work) have come under a lot of criticism because of the level of energy and electricity it takes to verify just one transaction. Your computer uses electricity, right? Have you experienced your computer's fans getting faster when you are playing an intense game right? Well, that is because the software demands more of the machine.

This is exactly the same with mining with PoW, it uses a whole lot of electricity that is contributing to the carbon emissions to an ever-warming planet.

But a lot of cryptocurrencies are switching to POS, which is Proof of Stake. It cuts the electricity consumption to a fraction of the amount while still involving the same security that blockchain has grown so famous for.

Pros and Cons of Crypto

So what can cryptocurrency do for you? It is time to take a look at the various benefits, as well as problems that come with investing in the digital coin.

High Risk

High risks might seem like a disadvantage, but there is a saying, "The bigger the risk, the greater the rewards." So unlike other investments that often reap lower levels of returns, you will also have the opportunity of earning greater amounts of money over shorter periods of time. Prices are driven through the demand and supply by those who are purchasing them. And because of this demand, it can result in some pretty big returns.

The Blockchain Tech That Runs Crypto is Highly Secure

Cryptocurrencies are not linked to the currencies themselves. One of the benefits of blockchain is the fact that no singular individual or small group of people actually would have control of blockchain or the cryptocurrency. And once you make a transaction on the blockchain, that record is permanent, and can never be erased. What this means is that people cannot tamper or change the information they are working with. No hacker can access and change the information on it without it easily being discovered.

A More Transparent Financial System

The truth is, very few people trust banks. And the majority of the financial systems work around third-party intermediaries who are busy processing all the different transactions. Think about it, the majority, if not all of us, have bank accounts. Whenever we pay for something online, or make use of our cards, we are making use of a third-party system. The same accounts for when we are making transactions online. It means that you are always placing your money and our trust into various intermediaries, and people are wondering, especially now, how good of an idea this is. Consider that if an intermediary's online system is offline, if only for an hour, could cause havoc. Payments and emergency funding can cause both panic and remind everyone of the reality that they never have full control of their own money.

This is where blockchain and cryptocurrencies do come in. Blockchain and crypto offer an alternative, where they can be viewed by everyone, and you are always in control of your money.

This kind of control can be seen as very appealing, especially after the recession within the early 2000s.

24/7 Trading

Normal stock markets often open and close within specific hours. That means the time you have to trade and work is limited. However, cryptocurrency markets are open 24/7, which means that you do not have to wait for exchanges to open. Unless you are working with brokers, then the time might be limited. So it means that you will be able to generate returns beyond your normal working hours.

Beats Inflation

In this economic day and age, inflation is a huge issue when it comes to saving and setting your money aside. But because crypto is not tied to the normal currencies or money run by the government, it means that inflation does not work with crypto. This is because a large number of crypto coins are capped/limited, which means that that amount of cryptocurrency cannot spiral out of control, which in turn will fix the inflation.

Volatility

You will always be hearing this from everyone investing in crypto, and every truthful book and article about cryptocurrency will not be failing to mention this. There are over 10,000 different cryptocurrencies in the market, and each have their own design and quirk. But they are all driven by price hikes and dives in the market.

Cryptocurrencies are called a volatile investment. This means the price of the coin will keep dropping and rising, and anything, even a Tweet from a celeb, can have an influence on the crypto's price.

So as you jump into crypto, you need to understand that it is going to be facing unpredictable price hikes and drops. You are going to have to learn to monitor the news, watch out for trends, and set bots in place that can pull you automatically from the market.

Cryptocurrency Does Take A Good Amount of Time and Effort

This means it can take a good, long while just to wrap your head around cryptocurrency. If you are still new to the digital world, then cryptocurrency and blockchain can feel a little like second nature. Although there are plenty of resources available, it takes a good amount of time and dedication to work wisely with cryptocurrency.

Cryptocurrency Is an Infantile Investment

Cryptocurrency has not been around for long, not like many different stocks, companies, and paper currencies (that have been around for centuries). That means that although they are widely known and keep growing in popularity, they lack history. People are still learning about this new concept, and do not have the centuries of histories like their neighboring investing assets. So, the scary truth? No one's really sure about what is going to happen with cryptocurrencies in the future. It means you need to be brave to enter the investing arena, where even experts are baffled by the flow and direction of the crypto market. So you won't always be able to rely on experts to have the right answers on the crypto market when they are still learning themselves.

Cryptocurrencies and Scalability

Scalability is the ability of something to adapt to growing. For example, if you have a train, once more people start taking the train, you can add more carriages to it in order to make space for more people to ride on the trains. That means a train is scalable. But cryptocurrency, despite its popularity, is still very small. They will run into issues if they are rolled out on a very large scale, including the time and rate that transactions are going to be processed.

Being New to Crypto Makes You Vulnerable

Cryptocurrencies may not have a whole lot of risks when it comes to banks and intermediaries, but because it is online, they are not completely free of various issues. As a crypto owner, you will come face to face with the possibilities of hackers, scammers, and even just being forgetful. If you lose your private key, you will lose all your access to your coins, and that is then game over. So you have to be on guard when it comes to crypto, because if you lose your cryptocurrency online, the chances of you getting it back is absolutely minimal.

So when you walk into cryptocurrency, you really have to be careful. It is a fine balance, much like working with a sharp instrument or building a fire. It can bring many great advantages or rewards to your door, but you have to play by certain rules and practice caution.

Chapter 3: Understanding NFTs

NFTs share the blockchain with cryptocurrency. But from then on, it is quite radically different. And there was a sudden explosion in popularity. NFTs are shown in the spotlight, but very few people really even understand what NFTs are.

But NFTs, unlike cryptocurrencies blockchain, are actually very easy to understand.

Introduction to NFTs

First of all, NFT stands for non-fungible token. Again, this term is really overly complicated.

But at the same time, it describes an NFT perfectly.

I'll explain.

"Non-fungible" means that it is very unique and irreplaceable. This would be something like a diamond. No diamond is the same or would hold the exact same value. Or another, perhaps simpler example, a zebra stripe or fingerprint.

‘Fungible’ means naturally that there are copies of the same thing. For example, a dollar bill. If you swap out a dollar bill for another dollar bill, you will be swapping the exact same thing. You will be able to buy the exact same thing. The only thing that will be different is the fact that you spent an extra five seconds swapping out a dollar bill for no apparent reason.

So going back to NFT, or the non-fungible token, is a digital file that has been permanently sealed on a digital level. They are a part of the blockchain, and are supported by the blockchain, but each token is completely unique.

So it can literally be anything digital. It can be a picture of melted ice cream, it can be a tweet you sent out last Friday, or it can even be a video of an animated tennis ball. Anything that you can place digitally can be an NFT.

You will just need to convert it into an NFT first.

And people buy NFTs?

Pretty much.

You can consider NFTs to work a lot like trading cards or authentic original artworks. This might be a bizarre example but imagine if the Starry Night by Vincent Van Gogh artwork were actually for sale. It is worth over $100 million dollars. That is quite a penny.

Now imagine if someone were to try and sell you a copy of the same artwork. You know there are hundreds of digital and printed copies of the Starry Night out there in the world. So will you pay $100 million dollars for a copy of the internet?

Didn't think so, but a person would for the authentic original painting.

That is how NFTs work. It gives the owner the original digital copy and rights. This is just on a virtual level. And the beauty about this is the fact that digitally, it cannot be destroyed.

NFTs have brought a rise to popularity within the digital art world. Where art collection is not only available now on a physical, but digital level.

Sure, you can try and sell a tweet, but unless you are the founder of twitter or a celeb, and have a huge platform, I don't think that is where you are going to be getting a whole lot of money from.

But you may wonder, why should you buy a video by Grimes for over $390,000 when you can download the exact same video from another site? You can get a digital copy of these works, right?

Yes, right, and that is why we go back to the Starry Night by Vincent Van Gogh. Only one authentic original version of the digital file exists. And when someone pays for it, as an NFT, then it gives it to them.

But I have to admit, it is a little bit of a gray blurry area. But if you can invest and make good money in this aspect, maybe you don't have to worry so much about all the digital technicalities. After all, everyone is still trying to figure out the digital future, there's bound to be a thing or two where we are left scratching our heads.

And when it comes to digital currency and NFTs, I have found myself scratching my head a lot.

Pros and Cons of NFTs

So what are the pros and cons of getting involved with NFTs? Well, there are a few things NFTs do bring to the table that are different from their crypto cousins, and therefore should naturally be addressed.

Pros:

- NFTs have the potential of growing in value. When you buy a token, or sometimes even simply earn a token, it has the potential of skyrocketing in value. For example, Cryptopunks that were originally given away for free can be sold for a couple of thousand dollars.
- Owning an NFT means you are holding onto something that is completely irreplaceable. And you have to admit, there is a good feeling that comes with that, as well as having bragging rights. It has many similarities as to holding on to a unique, one of a kind trading card. And who doesn't like showing off items that other people

can never have unless they buy it from you? Just me? Ok.

- Excitement and potential. NFTs are likely to be a part of a much bigger future. Many believe that the technology behind NFTs is going to change consumer behavior, much like the invention of the internet has. It is certainly an exciting idea that as you purchase an NFT, you start to take part in the future and technological evolution.
- Data records and transparency, you can now have official chain-of-ownership for an artwork without a struggle. The existing blockchain will have clear records of ownership for all NFTs, which means, on a theoretical basis, you would never need to have its authenticity questioned. Transparency builds a better platform of trust for people.

But there is a darker side to this coin. No system is perfect, and NFTs have their flaws. It just brings the question: are the benefits worth the risks?

- A person cannot digitize physical art, and there is an allure to be able to see a unique, one-of-a-kind painting that NFT tokens will be incapable of providing.
- NFTs are still quite confusing, and that means just because you are purchasing an NFT, does not mean you are purchasing the copyright to the art. What on earth does this mean? It means that you need to be careful of what NFTs you are buying and who you are buying it from. Also,

even if you own the copyrights, there is nothing stopping people from finding copies on the web and pasting it on social media. Basically, showing off and sharing the work that you paid thousands to even millions of dollars for. When you buy an asset online, it means you own the original asset, which brings to question, how much value is there truly over an asset that you don't have much control of? This is the digital murky waters that is bound to solve itself some or other time.

- Environmental impact, and unfortunately it has come to light that NFT has been a hot topic of debate when it comes to matters of the climate. Considering everyone is becoming painfully aware of climate change, it should come to your attention that Ethereum's blockchain requires huge amounts of NFTs. The same can be said that the trading of NFT and various other assets of blockchain is not a very environmentally friendly process. So if you are wise, you will always keep an eye out for NFTs impact on the environment, and the steps people are taking to make it more environmentally friendly.

NFTs bring so many unique, but confusing, matters to the table. Which brings to question, how exactly does one go about working and selling NFTs?

Chapter 4: How to Make Money with NFTs

How do you make money with NFTs? There are two important key aspects to answer that:

- Mastering the trends
- Building a community

Being able to identify and pick up on the trends that come with the NFTs are as important as building a community where you are going to sell your NFTs. There are different paths you can take to making money from NFTs, and it does not all involve you becoming an art prodigy and selling your work online.

However, that is one of the most popular tactics that people are starting to earn money with NFTs at this point.

And because of the massive competition, the fact of the matter is, you need to build yourself a loyal community that will trust and support your good word.

How To Make Money with NFTs

First, if you are a digital creator and have some creations you wish to make money from, then you can make an income by selling them as NFTs. Keep in mind, it's a little more than signing up to a market, uploading your work, and boom, you're rich. Especially if you are a beginner, you will be facing thousands of other artists and people who are just as interested in selling their NFTs as you are.

You can focus on making digital art, music, videos, memes, and audio clips. So you are really only limited by your imagination.

But you've got a lot of competition. So building up a community is incredibly important in order for this to even work.

Instead of making NFTs, you can also focus on trading and investing in them. This is when you buy NFTs that have shown to have a whole lot of potential, wait for a period of time then flip and sell them for a profit. This means you will have to take on the role as a collector, understanding the piece that you want to sell, and pick up when would be a good time to sell.

NFT gaming is starting to steal the show, where there are games when you can literally play to earn. Blockchain-based games are allowing you to purchase in-game items with the use of NFTs and trade them as well. You can earn NFTs in the game, or simply with giveaways or rewards for participating in discord groups, etc. For example, a game that has really proven it works would be Crypto Kitties. One single crypto kitty had managed to fetch around $300,000. Crypto Kitties is an NFT game that focuses on trading, breeding, and taking care of digital kitties.

You can also stake NFTs. What on earth is a stake? Whenever I hear this word, I think of either the juicy steak you could have with a glass of wine, or the staking of a vampire in different fantasy stories. But staking in the NFT community refers to storing your digital asset into a form of a 'stake', and in return, the community will give you a share of the world. One of the sites that offers this service would be Rplanet.

Another way you can make money through an NFT in a more indirect way would be to invest in the startups. NFTs have by now proven to be more than a quick crypto trend just passing by. They have started to show various logical and practical applications for various industries in the world. That means, new NFT startups are starting to pop up, and there is a whole lot of potential for investing in them for the future.

*Tip: for anyone selling their NFT, and it is their own original artwork, it is also possible for you to organize on your smart contract to receive a percentage of royalties whenever you have your artwork resold. This means that each time someone decides to sell your artwork again at a higher rate, then you will be receiving a constant small percentage of income. This is a very handy form of passive income that can come your way.

Building up a Community

The biggest factor that comes with making money with NFTs is building up yourself an online community. This is a sorely neglected fact when people talk about NFTs. But online communities allow you to build trust, verify yourself as an artist or simply an NFT trader, and add value to your NFT.

Basically, the more people like you online, the more valuable your NFTs become. It works a whole lot like Hollywood celebrities. The more a celebrity is liked, the more they get paid to be featured in movies, ads, and more.

And when people are going to be spending money on your artwork, you need to give them a reason. Even if it is over the fact that they like your artwork.

So what exactly is an online community? This is a group online that interacts with each other online for a specific reason or purpose.

In order to build a good community, you will have to build a great social network platform, and here are the top steps into achieving this:

- Find out your target audience and understand your community. You want to pay attention in this phase. You want to develop a great social network based on the parameters and values of your target audience. Who follows the different types of NFTs? What are your other interests? What is your unique approach that will appeal to them?
- Online research, make use of good AdWords, dig as deep as you need to go. The online research can take a lot of time, but it is really reliable and quite simple to do. Which is absolutely necessary when building an online community.
- Test and learn, you will be preparing a demo version of the social media and test it out on real people. See their reactions, arrange questions, and take your time. This might cost you a little, but it will be well worth your while.
- Develop a strategy of growth that is based on your users. You are competing against others looking for attention, so you will need to build a growth strategy. Start small, and start with one social media platform, and grow.
- Master the platform, the best way for you to use social media is if you know how to use the tools properly. So pick one specific social media platform where you know your target audience often spends time on, and keep growing and building.

You will also want to master:

- An SEO strategy
- Lead Generation Tactics
- Building a second social media platform

Having a community and building up a platform for yourself is even more important than the actual listing and selling of an NFT. This is purely because you need to make yourself visible in the markets. Otherwise, if you list your NFT, it will get drowned out by the thousands of others screaming for the same attention.

You don't necessarily have to make your scream louder.

Just make it more unique.

Imagine if you were in a crowded market, where everyone is trying to sell a different phone, then you suddenly heard the loud crows of a chicken. That is bound to attract attention, isn't it?

Basically, you want to take on an approach that resonates with the people but stands out from the rest.

That...is going to be tough.

But if you take some time doing your research, studying marketing, and spending time on social media, you will soon master the art of building your platform and community.

Chapter 5: Understanding Stocks

Stocks take a step out of the world of decentralized finance, and into the more common financial markets. Working with stocks is little different to working with cryptocurrencies. There is a little less risk involved and should certainly be considered when you start investing.

Introduction to Stocks

What exactly are stocks? Stocks represent a small part or percentage of ownership in a country. That when you are purchasing a stock, you are buying a small part, very small part, of ownership for that company. This is often called a share.

Investors love to purchase stocks in companies that they believe will be going up in value. If that does occur, then the stock's value, which means that when investors sell the stock again, they will be making a problem. But that is not the only benefit of stocks.

Pros and Cons of Stocks Explained

So, what can you get out of investing in stocks? Here are a few things to consider:

- First of all, you will be taking advantage of an economy that is growing. If the economy is growing, then so are the earnings within the corporate sector. You will want to benefit from the growth in more than just your average paycheck.
- Investing in stocks is one of the best ways to beat inflation. Stocks, as a norm, have always generally yielded fair levels of returns. These levels of returns are very often well beyond inflation. Which means, considering you beat the inflation, you are earning passive income.
- Stocks are also easy to buy shares from companies. You just need to find the right brokers, online platform, or financial planner. Once you have gone through the original hassle of setting up an account, buying the stock can take a matter of minutes.
- You don't have to break your back or budget when it comes to buying stocks. Buying stocks is not expensive, and some accounts such as Fidelity, do not have account minimums. If you are interested in buying certain company stocks, but they may be too expensive, you can also

consider buying fractional shares if your broker allows this type of investment.

- You will be making money in two ways when you are working with stocks. For one, you will be buying stocks at a lower price and selling it at a higher price. The other reality is that a lot of companies give dividends to people who hold onto stocks. That means you can earn a moderate form of passive income through stocks, and certain companies do have the habit of being more generous with the dividend, as it is an incentive for people to invest.

But what is the flipside to investing in stocks?

- There is still a degree of risk you cannot get rid of when you are currently investing in stocks. It means there is always the possibility that you would risk losing your entire investment. However, the risks involved in regular stock compared to cryptocurrency and NFTs are radically different and reduced. But, again, the risk will never be completely gone.
- Common stockholders are always paid last if a company were to go broke. That means, people who are preferred stockholders, bondholders, and any creditors are always going to be getting their money first if a company goes broke. Then, if there is anything left, you might receive your money, but I wouldn't get too optimistic.
- Time, investing in stocks requires a good amount of time, specifically time to do research

in the companies you are interested in. You will want to learn how to read financial statements, as well as various annual reports, in order to make the best decisions when it comes to choosing your companies. Because you do not want to invest in companies that you do not understand. It opens the opportunity of missing red flags or indicators of when you need to pull out of the market or should not have even invested in the first place.

- Emotional reality, this can be applied to investing in crypto and NFTs but investing in stocks can also add an emotional toll that most people are not truly prepared for. Majority of people may claim to deal with loss in a mature and strategic way, that is until you see your money go down the drain. Talking versus the actual reality is quite different. So you need to prepare yourself for this. Remember that if you really need to, take a step back out and away from investing until you have calmed yourself down.

Diversifying the Risk

One way you can take on risks with stock is by spreading out your investment types. You can and should apply this to crypto and NFT investments as well:

- Divide your investment stock through different investment types. You want to mix your investments between stocks, crypto, NFTs, and even other possibilities such as bonds or commodities. This is really the best way to invest. Start off with one category and learn as much as you can about that. Once you are confident of your investing abilities, add another category for your investments.
- You want to divide your stock investments through the different company sizes:
    - Small-cap
    - Mid-cap
    - Large-cap
- You will also want to check out and invest via location. For example, certain economies are faring better in certain countries than perhaps the one you are in or vice versa. Investing in different companies in different locations really helps to spread the risks and takes advantage of the growth without being vulnerable to any specific single geography.
- You also need to consider mutual funds and ETFs. These are groups that allow you to own hundreds of stocks even though you make just one purchase. These stocks are often selected by a professional fund manager. This is perhaps the easiest form of investments, and safest.

Chapter 6: Understanding Investment and Trading Strategies and Mistakes

Mistakes are all a part of life, but sometimes mistakes can come at a cost, and this is what you really want to avoid when your own money is at fault. I have learned that knowledge is learning from your own mistakes, and wisdom is learning from the mistakes of others.

People have walked this journey before and have very kindly shared some of the most common mistakes beginners have made. So it would be good to check it out, and be cautious yourself when you see the possibility of making the exact same mistake.

No Patience

Focusing on having a slow and steady approach when building your portfolio will bring greater rewards in the long run. But in a society that focuses on instant gratification, people want to see results today and lack the patience to plan and work ahead. You need to learn to set realistic expectations for yourself.

Falling in Love with A Coin, NFT, or Market

This makes me think of Dogecoin, and its prime reason for popularity is because of community loyalty, but it does not provide as many advantages or factors to the table that many other cryptocurrencies have. You might also find yourself particularly attached to an NFT or to a company with which you have bought shares. There is nothing wrong with enjoying company or appreciating a coin. However, you need to be willing to consider selling if you see fundamental changes indicating that you need to change direction. Sticking with an investment based on pure loyalty (even if you have no direct connections to the company, NFT or business) should make you realize that you don't have to stay overtly loyal to the investment. You need to stay loyal to the trends, as well as what the other charts are telling you.

Not Doing Enough Research or Understanding the Investment

I was horrified to learn how ignorant people can be at some point when they have the ability to learn about it with a simple tap on one's phone. We are in a scary era, where we have access to information, but do not use it as we should. Not enough investors do enough research when it comes to matters of what they are buying into.

Always go the extra mile when choosing your investments. You would much rather want to play it safe than sorry, and so spending just a little extra time to find out everything you want and need to know before making any kinds of decisions. Because even if you were to buy and back out quickly, you will still have to deal with transaction fees, which means you will still be dealing with a loss.

Forgetting to Diversify

If an investment is doing really well, it may be tempting to pour all you have into it. But this is a mistake, and every savvy investor will not support the idea of placing all your eggs into a basket. It is wiser, always wiser, to stick to the principle of diversification. Why? Well, think about it. Sure, the investment you are doing is currently doing very well. But if these last few years have taught us anything, it is how unpredictable life can be. If the investment were to swing in a totally different direction, you will lose everything.

Yes, does that mean you won't always make as much money as you would like to? Absolutely, but this is a matter of wisdom and risk management.

Emotional Power

It has been mentioned that stocks, cryptocurrency, and NFTs can have an emotional toll. And truth be told, whenever you work with money, it is going to be messing with your head. And the biggest mistake you can make is allowing emotion to control you. It would not be a far-fetch to say that emotion is the no.1 killer to your returns in investments.

And please do not think that you will not be affected. You are a human, not AI, and with that means you have emotions and feelings. You might struggle less, or you might struggle more, but it is still going to be a struggle. So do yourself a favor and start studying trading psychology before stepping into the market.

The idea of trading psychology is mentally preparing yourself for the emotions that you are going to be dealing with. So when you might be heading towards an emotional pitfall, you will be able to identify and work against it. The biggest issue with emotions is the lack of recognition of how much it can control you and your choices..

The problem is the market works on brutal logic and supply and demand alone, and so the choices you make have to be logical and strategic as well.

Waiting for the Opportunity of Getting Even

So you have gotten a knock on the market, the prices are lower in your investment, and you decide to ride the wave and wait until the market picks up again. However, the market is not showing any indications of recovery, and you are simply losing any profit that you might have actually received. This is actually called a “cognitive error” according to behavioral finance, and you lose out in two ways. By waiting before selling a losing investment, it can carry on until the investment might actually become worthless. And you lose out on opportunity cost. Basically, the money you could have gotten back could have been placed in better use.

Investment Turnover

Investment turnover has also been seen as a form of return killer. Where you are only receiving low commission rates, but being eaten alive by transaction costs, because you are constantly jumping in and out of commissions. This certainly counts for cryptocurrency investments and NFTs as the platforms you can buy and sell them do charge very specific fees.

Trying to Time the Market

Perfect timing only happens by accident, and when you time the market, it is also going to kill returns. Even the savviest of investors do fail to pull this off successfully, which means that trying to find the perfect timing of entering and exiting the market might cost you more than what is worth your while.

How to Avoid Most of These Mistakes

You can start off by setting aside time to develop an action plan for yourself. You want to determine how much you want to spend, and how much you want to earn, and the time it should take to get there. By the end of the year, you need to review your investments and how well they have performed according to your expectations.

As your income is constantly growing, then you want to consider adding more. You might even want to participate in compounding interest. This is when you put your returns straight back into the investment, which means that you earn a greater percentage as time goes on. This is often called a "snowball effect."

Remember that mistakes are all going to be a part of the process. You won't be able to escape mistakes. It's like telling a tennis player they are never going to miss a ball or telling a video gamer that they are never going to fail a level.

If you can avoid as many of them as possible, you will reduce the losses you are going to be facing in the future. Also, if you learn to quickly move on or take a day off and a step back when making a mistake can prevent yourself from diving into even more mistakes.

Because a person, once stressed, is far more likely to make mistakes when they are in emotional distress from their previous mistakes.

Investment Strategies

So what are the most common strategies you can take on when it comes to cryptocurrencies, NFTs, and stocks?

Well, investing mostly involves identifying a good investment, buying it, holding on to it until a good opportunity arrives, and selling it again. When it comes to stocks, a lot less monitoring will be needed in comparison to crypto and NFTs.

But you can also adopt the Dollar-Costing-Average strategy.

Dollar cost averaging, also known as DCA, is a strategy to lower the amount of money you are paying for investments, and reduce the risks involved. Instead of purchasing all the shares at a specific price point, you will be dividing the amount of money you plan to spend and buy in small but regular intervals. It doesn't matter what the price is.

This strategy helps you manage risk and is especially effective for volatile investments.

An example would be if you decided to buy $10,000 worth of Bitcoin. You divide it into $1,000 for 10 weeks. You will then buy $1,000 worth of Bitcoin every Wednesday at 14:00. You will then end up with far more Bitcoin than if you bought $10,000 worth of Bitcoin in one go.

This strategy might also be more affordable for you. Where the majority of people do not altogether have $10,000 that they can scoop out and invest in Bitcoin in one go.

The reason why DCA works so well is because over the long term, asset prices tend to rise, but they do not do so over the short term. As a matter of fact, they tend to run into various highs and lows that do not follow any sort of predictable pattern. And following this strategy is going to garner greater success than attempting to time the markets.

DCA also helps to remove a whole lot of the emotion of the investing, as you have to purchase a small amount on a regular basis. It helps those who have less to invest and is a relatively simple strategy. You don't have to worry about overly complicated timing.

Does Dollar Cost Average Work?

It's a strategy, which means it may not play out as neatly as it could. It works better for more volatile investments, where the prices keep jumping up and down. However, for the very long-term, the DCA strategy can cause an underperformance. So if you do happen to have a large sum of money, it might work out better if you invest sooner than later.

DCA does help your money to grow, and because of the impossibility to predict the future, this strategy has been shown to offer solid risks while reducing the risks.

You should consider using Dollar Cost Averaging if you:

- Are just starting to invest, and only have the capabilities of buying smaller amounts of shares.
- Not interested in going in depth research of market timing.
- Want to make regular investments into retirement accounts.
- Not planning to invest in down markets.

If you, however, want the following, you might need to consider a different strategy:

- If you are only planning on investing for the short term.

- If you are trying to enjoy your time on the market and do not mind spending extra time doing your research and learning how to work the markets.
- You have quite a large amount of money you want to invest.
- You want to invest in mutual funds that require higher minimals through a brokerage account that is taxable.

DCA is a perfect strategy for beginners, and if you have the goal of investing for the long term.

Common Trading Beginner Strategies

Before we dive into trading strategies, you will need to learn how to read a trading chart. When you are working for more short-term strategies, you need to learn how to read a chart. When it comes to cryptocurrency, you will want to learn about the Japanese candlestick chart. This is because the amount of information that is shared in a candlestick chart is more than enough for you to pick up on trends, when to enter and leave the market.

Majority of platforms also offer for you to see the information in the candlestick charts.

The Candlestick charts originally come from Japan, 100 years before the West had developed point and figure/bar chats. In the 1700s, there was a Japanese man by the name of Homma, who had discovered the link between the price and the supply and demand of rice, and that a lot of the markets held a very strong sway by the emotions of those who were trading.

Much like a bar chart, candlestick charts show the opening of a market and the close price. They are also color coded. That means if the candlestick is green, then the closing price is higher than its opening price.

If it is red, then the closing price is lower than its opening price.

The candlestick's timeline can also be adjusted.

And if the upper shadow of the candle on the bottom is short, it is an indication that during its opening time it was closer to the price high (the price rise). When the shadow is closer at the top or end of the candle, it means the price hike (high) was closer at the end of the candle.

This can literally range between a couple of minutes, hours, days, weeks to even months.

The candlesticks are created so that you can see the up and down movements of the price. It means that although the price movements may appear random, you will be able to pick up on trends and a general direction of the price.

Patterns are separated between bullish and bearish.

Bearish patterns are an indication when the candlesticks are heading in an upward direction. This means that the amount of sellers in the market outnumber the buyers. The pattern indicates that the price will continue to decline.

Bullish patterns occur when there are more sellers than there are more buyers. When bulls have taken over on the candlestick chart, the price could be in a higher direction.

Then there is the bearish evening star. This occurs when the last candle pattern open is below the previous day's small real body. This pattern shows that buyers are slowing down and sellers are trying to take control of the market.

*Tip: climb onto your search engine and look up instances of bearish patterns on candlestick charts and bullish patterns on the chart. Finish off with checking out the bearish evening star. Because no matter how much I try to explain it to you here, you will need some form of visual representation in order to be able to identify it when you come across the live markets.

There are various other bullish and bearish patterns to study, those would include:

- Bearish Falling Three
- Bullish Rising Three
- Bullish Harami
- Bearish Harami cross

- Bearish Engulfing Pattern

Why is it important to learn these patterns? Well, when you want to implement short-term trading strategies, a lot of the strategies involve identifying trends on the charts in the live markets and applying a plan accordingly in order to earn money.

This may seem daunting because this does get technical.

So before practicing on the real markets, try paper trading first. Paper trading works like a simulation but removes all the risks. You can learn to master the charts, try out the different strategies, and gain confidence in the markets before even setting foot in the live markets.

This is something you really should consider especially as a beginner. Maybe taking on a long-term investment strategy while you practice and try your hand out in the simulations.

News Trading Strategy

This is a strategy that involves watching the news and the market expectations based on the news releases. Considering how dependent crypto is on people's opinions, this is a good strategy to consider.

What are some things you need to consider?

- Has the news been fully factored in the price of an instrument or only have been partially priced in?
- Is the news currently matching the market expectations?

Here are some tips you should follow:

- You need to treat each market and news release individually.
- You need to develop strategies for specific news releases.
- The expectation on the markets and the reaction of the markets are both more important than the news releases themselves.

Trading works a lot on the news releases, and traders need to understand how exactly the financial workers function. So you need to spend a lot of time monitoring the news and watching the market's reaction before jumping into anything. There is a common trading motto shared: "It is better to travel than to have arrived."

This means that it is better to trade on the action of the price before an announcement has been made, rather than waiting for the announcement to arrive. This protects traders from a certainty level of volatility from the one thing more effective than the actual news forecast: rumors.

Yes, rumors, gossip, and guesses. You need to learn to buy the rumor and sell the news strategy.

The benefit is that you have solid enter and exit strategies where you base your trade on how exactly the market is interpreting the news. This is quite tricky to learn, but soon you will see and connect the dots on the flow of the market in comparison to the flow of the market.

You will also be able to identify various trade opportunities. Having the choices allows you to sit back and learn. You won't have to suffer from FOMO (fear of missing out), because you understand that there will always be another opportunity.

However, this form of trading holds a lot of overnight risk. It means that if you haven't left any positions, you are at risk.

And news trading requires quite a high level of skills. You do not want to be falling under the trap of listening to what people are telling you, but rather want to identify the trends, and what the news are saying. This can be tricky. A lot of mistakes can be made. Which is why you should consider trying out a few rounds of paper trading, where the simulation is a copy of the live markets. This is an excellent platform to practice this strategy before trying your hand at it in the live markets. This strategy leaves gaping space for a whole lot of mistakes, so you want to do what you can to master it before incurring a great amount of loss.

End-of-day Trading Strategy

This end of day strategy is focused on trading close to the end of markets. This is naturally a strategy that involves the stocks, and not the 24/7 crypto or NFTs. This strategy requires a whole lot of price action in comparison to the previous day's movements in price.

End-of-day traders focus on how much the price could move based on the price action and indicators placed on the system. Normally, risk management is set up, where traders place a stop-loss order, a limit order, and a take-profit order to reduce the risks of trading overnight.

*Tip: stop-loss orders need to become your new best friend when it comes to the trading world. This is when an AI monitors the price movement, and if the prices were to drop while you are not watching, the AI pulls you out of the market before too much of a loss has been made. This is especially important for volatile and fluctuating markets. So if you like working with risky investments, then you have to be best friends with stop-loss.

End-of-day trading is most suitable for most types of traders and can be a good trick to start your trading journey.

There is also a reduction in time commitments. You will either be placing your order in the morning or at night, so the time it takes is comparatively less than various other strategies.

But there are still a whole lot of overnight risks, which means you need to place in guaranteed stop-losses.

Swing Trading Strategy

This occurs when an investor has the goal of buying security when they expect the market will rise and sell when they expect the price to fall. Swing trading is a very technical approach on the markets and requires a lot of experience reading the charts and analyzing the bigger movements.

Swing trading is successful when you learn to interpret the length and duration within each swing. These swings are defined through the support and resistance levels. Traders also learn how to identify the increasing levels of both supply and demand.

- You want to use a pattern recognition scanner to help you identify the technical analysis on a chart.

Swing trading, however, works better as a hobby, and is suitable for people who have limited time. It does require prior experience and understanding of how the patterns work. Swing strategies can also work both ways.

However, it does contain overnight risks, and requires a whole lot of research. The more analysis that is needed, the bigger chances there are of you possibly getting it wrong. So you want to be cautious. Swing trading should also be practiced on paper trading first before implementing it in the field.

Day Trading Strategy

With day trading, you are actively trading during the day, and close off when the markets close. This strategy is cool if you are interested in making trading a full-time profession. Day traders take advantage of the various fluctuations in the market, and only hold their positions for the day. This removes the risks of the overnight markets, and day traders are required to have an organized trading plan which is quickly adaptable.

Benefits of day trading involve the fact that there are very little overnight risks and limited intra day risks. It means that because an average trade lasts around 1-4 hours, this reduces risks that occur during longer-term trades. Time flexible trading also happens for those who want flexibility for trading. Normally a trader might enter 1-5 different positions that are occurring during the day.

However, day trading requires a lot of self discipline. It requires you to be able to pre-determine strategies, learn to stick with it, manage risks, and call it a day when need be. Some trades might turn out flat as well, which means there are just some positions that are not going to be moved within the day, as expected.

There are a wide variety of other trading strategies available, and you want to choose ones that suit you best and really work for you.

And do not be discouraged if you counter some initial losses. Patience is key to becoming a successful trade, and mistakes and losses are just a part of growing your skills in investing.

Purchasing the Right NFT

And no, we are not forgetting about NFTs either. Although NFTs focus more on the buy and hold strategies, the key to earning money with NFTs is identifying the best NFTs and those who hold the most potential, holding onto it, and selling it once the price rises.

So here are top things to look out for when you want to buy an NFT.

Unique Properties Within the NFT

NFTs tend to come in the shape and form of collections. For example, the Bored Ape Yacht Club or Peaceful Groupies. If you think of Pinterest, you have a board where you have various pins. Works pretty much the same.

Now within these collections, some NFT properties have higher values, whereas some others do not. That means if you want to choose an NFT with the most value, you will want to check out the properties on an NFT.

It is also a good way to identify a scam account or make sure the NFT is legitimate. Because although scammers can upload copies or famous NFTs, they cannot make an exact replica of the properties. So it is an extra safety measure you can take on before you go ahead and buy an NFT.

Seller Verification

Much like Twitter and Instagram, there are many sellers on the OpenSea platform that also have a blue verification tick on well-known NFT artists. It proves that they are trusted and not accounts of impersonators. Now that does not mean you should just buy from people who have the blue tick, as that means you might miss out on some pretty lucrative opportunities, but the blue tick does help. You can also double check the account by checking out the seller's social media accounts. You can also make confirmation by checking out their sales states page or DMing them personally to confirm.

Market Platform Transaction Fees

You are often going to be charged a transaction fee when making purchases on a platform. This works for any commerce or online platform, and you will want to check out just exactly how much is going to be charged.

Some platforms charge fees on both ends of the transaction, such as with Rarible, and some of the fee goes to the sellers, like OpenSea. For the majority of exchanges, the fee goes to the sellers. But this is an extra cost you have to take into consideration, especially if you are working on a tight budget.

The Market Value and Liquidity of the Market

NFTs do not carry the same amount of liquidity as cryptocurrency does, which is important to always keep in mind. It means that you cannot quickly sell your NFT if need be, and this can cause hitches in your investment plans. Why? Well, if the market is swinging in a different direction, then you might not get your asset sold in time before it has a harmful impact. Cryptocurrency is known to be quite liquid, and therefore, leaving the market is a lot easier as well as entering the market.

The NFT market is still incredibly young. Considering that two years ago, barely anyone was talking about it, and now we are seeing artworks getting sold for millions. People are still warming up to NFTs and will continue to do so for the next upcoming years. It is going to take time for people to buy into NFTs, and even if they do, the future of the NFT markets is bound to look radically different from what we know and see today.

Price Performance with Sellers on Other NFTs

If you want to double check on the NFT you want to buy, and check to see if it is a good investment, then it would be a good idea to check out the seller's account. You can see their previous sales and see what their pieces are currently selling for. There is a beauty in the level of transparency within the NFTs market, which allows you to do more than enough market research to make smart choices on your purchases.

Accessibility and Rarity Distribution

NFT distributions need to be checked for how rare they are. They are normally categorized by ordinary, rare, or super rare.

Super rare NFTs are often deemed the most valuable, and they normally have a distribution of around 3%.

Rare distribution traditionally goes around 5 - 10%, as this is considered reasonable.

Ordinary NFTs are very common and can reach up to 85%-94%. Basically, they will be holding on to the least amount of value.

The Community

If you are an NFT seller, you need to build up a good community. As a buyer, you need to be a part of a good community. You want to check up and see how the company is focused on those participating on the projects, and how committed is the community in itself. If you find the community to be dead, then you need to steer very clear and far away. You want to be involved in NFT communities that are actively involved and goal oriented.

Market: Supply and Demand

Cryptocurrency runs on this, so do NFTs. The value of an NFT keeps increasing when the demand is increased. This happens through tactful advertising and marketing. So will the company running the NFT projects you are interested in be able to meet the supply and demand if the market were to surge. You want to look for a marketing strategy that is specifically tied to the number of NFTs within the collection. If you see clear reasoning and plans for the NFTs future and strategy, then you are looking at a good investment potential.

NFT Competition

There is a whole lot of irony that comes with this, but you need to take into consideration what other NFTs are out there. Investing in NFTs works a lot like running a business. You are checking out what is in demand, what is selling, trends, etc.

So you want to see how other communities are being run, whether or not they are staying on top of the trends, and how they are capturing the audience's attention. All these factors are what you would look for in a business.

Remember that NFTs are great opportunities for investment but remember to play it safe. You want to take every factor mentioned here into consideration before making any purchases. Impulse spending must not exist within the realms of NFTs, that is just too much of a risk.

Chapter 7: Understanding Tools and Tricks to Help Your Journey

The online platform is constantly evolving, and people are out there making use of so many different software, tools, and tricks to enjoy. This involves both NFTs, stocks, and cryptocurrencies.

Many of these tools are available for free and bound to aid in your journey of overall success.

Paper Trading

As explained before, paper trading is a simulated trade. It allows you to practice buying and selling without putting any real money in the trade.

The term is coined from many years back, where people used to keep track of all their trades on paper and would practice on paper before risking their money in the live markets. Fortunately, software has evolved to the point that you do not have to work everything out on paper.

Simulations work very closely to real life and will give you some foundational knowledge and confidence to move forward, try out new strategies and make mistakes in a safe environment. This is especially relevant for someone who wants to take on cryptocurrency. The fluctuating nature of crypto does call for more experience, and the best way you can get experience is by trying your hand out in paper trading.

Much like you practice swimming in a pool before trying out the ocean, and before you pilots learn on simulators before climbing on a real plane, paper trading has far more benefits that outweigh the cons paper trading.

Difference Between Paper Trading Versus Live Accounts

Paper trading could evoke a false sense of security, because the results you may receive on the paper trade simulation is not guaranteed to occur on the live markets. And because it removes the risks, that means that you will still have to deal with the overall emotional impact that you will be facing on the live markets.

So you will have to practice good trading psychology when you are in the live markets, as you will not be facing a lot of the emotional impact in the simulation.

Paper trading accounts do not factor in all the transaction fees and commissions that may be occurring in the live accounts. So you need to be lenient and flexible with your budgeting if you build a budget based on the paper trading platform.

Common Paper Trading Accounts for Crypto

TradingView

TradingView normally offers some of the best paper trading tools for you to try out. It is both very user-friendly and provides simple but comprehensive live charts. You will be able to find charts that involve crypto and regular markets within the Tradingview. This platform does offer you a trial for over 30 days, so you will have plenty of time checking out all the tools and features. There are also 3 paid plans: commonly called Premium, Pro+ plan, and paid plans.

You can also interact with the public and private chats.

Cryptohopper

Cryptohopper works a little differently than the other simulators on the internet. It is a little advanced. It works with a crypto trading bot, and if you are interested or leaning in to learn how the bot works, then this is a good start.

You can experiment with the trading strategies, and there are very few differences between the real trading platforms. Instead of having it connected to your exchange account, it is connected to the public data.

eToro

eToro is a very popular trading platform, and an online crypto broker platform that allows you a wide variety of different options. It has a great simulation platform, and even allows you to follow some of the top traders around.

When you practice with an eToro account, you will be getting free $100,000 trial/play money for practice.

There is also a great community built in the eToro community. Traders are gathering all around the world with various trade ideas, and as a newbie, you can follow expert investors on the platform, and you will even be able to follow their trading ideas. It gives you clean access to learning from the best.

StormGain

This is a very well built and comprehensive trading platform in the market. It also provides a great interface for simulations, and very user-friendly for anyone starting up, this is a very user-friendly platform.

*Tip: If you can find yourself a trading platform that offers paper trading on the side. It would be ideal, as you can both practice and familiarize yourself with the same platform. So once you have trained on the paper trading platform, you can simply revert to the live market on the same platform.

Best NFT Tools

With NFTs coming to the world in the shape of games, art, collectibles, and many more areas, it is always a good idea to keep an eye on the NFT space and see exactly where it is heading. There are tools that are being developed and have already come out that you can use for investing.

Nansen

This is a paid tool that is pretty pricey, but it has some of the best features for diving into the NFT space. You can see the wallet leaderboard and analyze what smart money is doing. Basically, it analyzes and tracks wallets and the market activity of NFTs on the Ethereum blockchain. It can pick up on trends and let you know of the best NFT possibilities out there.

Dune Analytics

This is a blockchain research tool, where you can build your very own dashboard and queries, is free for use, and gives you data provided from Ethereum, Binance Smart Chain, Polygon, Optimism, as well as the Gnosis Chain. Dune is a very powerful research tool where you can access various publicly available queries and dashboards. Basically, it is a tool that gives you access to a lot of information and communities.

Icy Tools

This is a very user-friendly platform, and it does come at a monthly cost. You will have lifetime access to NFTs that are available, be alerted to new potential alerts, a great community, and it is a fantastic learning resource for beginners.

It will also be showing all the trending collections and the real-time floors. You will be able to see the volume, floor price, and average sales price of NFTs.

You will also be able to buy lifetime memberships to ICY founder clubs.

Rarity Tools

Each NFT's rarity score will be listed here, very easy to use for beginners, and free to use. You will be able to use this tool to help you find all the potential and upcoming NFTs that have the potential of growing in value.

They will also be launching a mint calendar that will be updating you of the NFT projects that are launching.

OpenSea

This is the biggest NFT marketplace, and famous for the trading, selling, and the creation of NFTs. Open provides you with a wide variety of tracking and analyzing tools of NFTs, and supports Ethereum's, Polygon's, and Clayton's blockchain.

NFT Tools

Other NFT tools you can consider would be:

- NFT go
- SPR3ADSH33T's INSIGHTS
- Non-Fungal
- NFT STats
- NFT Nerds
- NFT Stats
- Super Sea Browser Plugin
- NFT Drop Calendar
- NFT catcher
- Zerion
- NFT Evening
- NFT Plaza

Top Crypto Toolkit

And cryptocurrency also has their fair share of tools. In fact, it is shocking to see all the tools a person has available, and naturally you can choose whichever one you like the most. But here is a small list to get you started.

Exchanges

Starting off, you need a good exchange, here is a list of some of the best exchanges to consider:

- Binance
- Binance.US
- Coinbase Pro
- BitMEX

If you want to try your hand at decentralized exchanges, there is:

- IDEX

*Tip: if you are new to cryptocurrencies, then it may be best to avoid decentralized exchanges. This is purely because centralized exchanges are far more user-friendly, have a much larger market, and you might not even be able to work on a decentralized platform, unless you already have cryptocurrencies which you bought of centralized exchanges (because you won't be able to connect your decentralized platform to your bank).

Trading Platforms

Trading platforms bring some of the best tools to table by streamlining it. Now you will be able to perform multiple different trades all on one platform:

- Coinigy
- Tradedash

Charting Tools

Charting tools are necessary to pick up on trends and implement different strategies. This tool will allow you to visualize different trading indicators. It can help you grow your skills in technical analysis (TA).

- Tradingview
- Cryptowat.ch

Market Data

You need access to real-time accurate information in order to make the best choices in a trade. So social media is out when it comes to market data. What can you use?

- Coinmarketcap
- OnChainFX

Calendar

Just like NFTs have their fair share of announcements, project drops, and news, cryptocurrency shares the different forks, swaps, block halving, and even airdrops.

- CoinMarketCal
- Condar

You also want to look at:

- Crypto Research Report
- CryptoPanic
- FAWS

These are platforms that give you detailed reports or news free of any aggregators (people who like to spread rumors to manipulate the market).

Best Digital Wallets

It is recommended that you have both a hot and cold wallet. What is a hot wallet? This is a wallet that works online, and you can easily have transactions done. However, this wallet is also the most insecure.

Cold wallets are stored normally in a hard drive and takes much longer to have transactions done. However, cold wallets are far more secure.

*Tip: do not lose your cold wallet password, as some of them do not have the reset password, which means if you lose your password, you lose everything.

Cold wallets are great for storing most of your crypto and NFTs you would like to set aside for a specific period of time. This is because cold wallets are practically 'hacker-proof'.

Consider it like having a bank and a wallet of cash on you in real life. You will be carrying a certain amount of cash to do your day to day expenditures, but most of your money is stored safely in a vault, tucked away.

Some good wallets are:

- MetaMask
- MEW
- Exodus
- Ledger Nano S

Chapter 8: Understanding Safety from Scammers and Risky Investments

The online community is just as precarious or, well, dangerous as the offline community. Instead of dark alleyways, a person has dodgy websites, and instead of lollipops or treats, they have links.

Basically, you need to practice caution when working online, and if you are working with crypto and NFTs, then it becomes especially important. Think about it this way, you put most of your money or valuables in some kind of safe or into the bank. Why? Because it is a lot safer there than walking around with it on your person.

What is worse about the online community is the fact that they have mastered the art of scamming and conning you into giving the information they need to steal from you.

But that is also where the tricky reality is. Majority of the hacks, scams, and cons that are pulled off are done so successfully if the hacker knocks on the 'computer's door' and the person with the computer 'opens' the door by clicking on a link, email, or typing in information on a website they thought they could trust.

So here are a few things to remember, especially when working online in order to stay safe. Think about it this way, five seconds of extra caution will save you five years worth of damage.

I had plenty of time, taking just that extra second or two to think a little more through. I have typed out messages scammers have sent me into a search bar to discover their ruse, and there is always one question I ask when someone online offers me "free stuff":

What are they getting out of this?

Understanding Scammers

Online scams work a little differently to the various other scams people have pulled off, but there are certain factors that scammers tend to fall back on, because it has the tendency to actually work.

- Start off by always checking the URLs before clicking on them. The web address/URL are one of the biggest giveaways as to whether or not something is a scam. This is because scammers love to build 'phishing' websites that can look nearly identical to the website you know. But there will always be one discrepancy, and that is going to be in the URL. There are some cases, however, where it may contain the right address, but also added code to reroute any forms of traffic to a false website. So if you see yourself leaving the page and entering a 'new one' whenever you need to fill in sensitive information, then it is time to check that URL address again.

- Always stay alert and always be skeptical, and this counts even if the messages or recommendations come from friends on social media. If people are contacting you on your phone or email asking for personal information, be suspicious, and only open links or attachments from emails that you trust. Even so, there are frequent cases of phishing emails, so just visiting the website directly (it might be a bit more of a hassle than a link but will save you from always entering the wrong one), then that is even highly recommended.
- Understand who your web host providers are for your internet, hosting, as well as emails. It is important to understand their security measures, as well as how they will be contacting you.

Common Tactics Scammers Use

Always be on the alert from these common tactics scammers use:

- Faking a possible emergency. Remember that although there might be an emergency of some kind with a company that you know, they will ALWAYS have the professional courtesy of giving you the time you need to respond and think things through. Scammers won't have that same courtesy. Scammers also love to pretend to be an official organization and demand immediate money for issues that are bogus. They will use terms and phrases such as "Your account will be frozen," or even "You could be fined $10,000." Basically, anything to stir up panic and cause you to jump into action before questioning the source. Again, professional companies give time, regardless of the emergency scenario, so take a deep breath when receiving such messages, and just take a closer look. Start researching and investigating.

- This comes in line with the first tactic, but scammers will not allow victims to hang-up the phone, normally by stating that there will not be a second chance to fix the problem. Now if this is coming from a business, where have you ever heard a true businessman say that you cannot come back? The same can be said with any company or institution that needs to resolve a situation with you. Scammers do not allow that professional courtesy, so the moment they tell you not to hang up is the moment red flags should be raised.
- They might even start by stating that they are not asking for any sorts of personal information–at the start. Asking for personal information always raises red flags for anyone to

let down their guards, but then they will use other tactics such as using gift cards to extract payments.

Remember that with scammers, they love to either scare their victim into giving them money or trick them into believing they have won something. So again, always be suspicious.

This is especially true on social media, which is the perfect platform for scammers of crypto. If anyone DM's you personally, stating they have free crypto to give away, or a lucrative tip for investing, BE SUSPICIOUS. Why? Well, who really goes out their way to contact a stranger online to share information that they would rather want to keep to themselves...unless, of course, they are a scammer?

Understanding Online Security

There are also times when hackers do not contact you directly but try other methods and tactics to get access to your computer or accounts and steal your stuff. So just like you would take your money to the bank, it is time to build your own personal digital vault to keep your information safe. This normally comes in a set of rules for you to follow that can really boost your security:

- Always use a different password for every single account. Because if you had the same password for different accounts, then they are all at risk if your hacker learns that password.
- Remember to keep installing your security updates on a regular basis. Malwares and viruses are constantly adapting, so your security needs to stay up to date in order to avoid being vulnerable for attacks.
- If you have the option for two-factor authentication, then use it, always. Because if a hacker gets a hold of your password for an account but doesn't have your phone or whatever else is used for your account, then they are still very much stuck.
- Always have an antivirus and always keep it up to date. Any device that can connect online needs to have an antivirus. This would include your mobile phone (majority of people forget that phones are far more vulnerable than computers to hacking). Also, if your anti-virus does not have this feature, be sure to get yourself a program against ransomware too.
- Make sure you explore and understand the different security tools that you are getting installed. The more you know about them, the better you can use them, right?
- If you can, get yourself a paid VPN and be sure to use it. VPN can hide your IP address and prevent them from stealing files or data through a network. However, the word PAID is being emphasized here, because free VPNs often sell

your information to make up for their 'free' services, or their services are just terrible quality.

- Even if they are just optional, make sure to use passcodes and passwords. It might be adding a small pain to your life, but you are adding extra security measurements against people who really want to use and steal information from you.
- Use different email addresses for the different kinds of activities you do online. This is a very methodical trick, where you keep your online identities separate. So if you receive an email about your bank on the email address you use for your social media, then you will certainly know it is fake.
- Clear your cache every now and then. Your browser is constantly storing information about you, and your web history can often lead to showing your family info, your address, and various other forms of personal information that you do not want any other person getting their hands on.
- Protect your privacy on social media. Everyone knows that when you make an account online, you are not the customer, you are the product. And when it comes to sharing matters online, it is all too easy to go about sharing too much. So be paranoid with what you share online, how much you share, and who everyone has access to. There are certainly sites like Facebook who have very intricate privacy settings. Be sure to

familiarize yourself with your privacy settings on social media, and always think twice before posting a video.

Understanding Risky Investments

So, what do you do to avoid NFT and crypto scams? Here are some steps you can take to avoid falling victim to NFT scams. Following the information above should already help prevent the majority of scammers, but there are some scams uniquely tailored to NFTs that people need to understand.

Common NFT Scams

- Phishing scams or pop-ups that are awfully suspicious. Sometimes, as you are purchasing your very first NFT, you will need to sign your wallet that makes transactions to the blockchain you are working on (most likely Ethereum), and MetaMask is one of the most popular wallets for Ethereum. However, recently some MetaMask users have been the target of phishing scams where there are advertisements asking for the private wallet keys. They tend to pop up via public forums, Discords, etc., providing a link to the supposedly normally login pages. I think you already understand where I am going with this. Never give your seed phrase to anyone, and always visit the verified website directly.

- Fake personas and catfishing, considering that all the marketing will be occurring on social media, catfishing is very popular then too. Popular NFT communities have the habit of hiring influencers, as well as celebs to promote them, but this makes it difficult to determine which NFTS are real or not.
- Look out for Pump-and Dump schemes. This is when a group of people buys the NFTs or the currency and causes the price to soar up. Then they hype it up online as well, putting all effort to drive up the value of the crypto or the NFT. Once they have garnered success, they cash out and leave behind worthless assets and a hefty loss for everyone else who was involved. In order to avoid this, always go checking the history and wallet records of the projects that catch your eye. Transparency is key, and you will be able to see if there are discrepancies with the sudden price hikes.
- Bidding scams occur when you have purchased an NFT and now want to resell it to the person who bids the highest. But the problem is once you list your NFT, the bidders will change the cryptocurrency they are using without letting you know. So before you accept any bid, double check the currency, and never accept a bid that is lower than what you want (for a minimum).

- Also, remember that when you mint an artwork, it is not exactly the same as having the intellectual property/ownership of the work. And OpenSea's software can turn any image or digital file into an NFT, regardless of whether or not they have the rights. So scammers steal artist's work and open fake OpenSea accounts–selling counterfeit artwork that, in essence, has no value. So before making any form or purchase of an NFT, always check to see if you are buying from a verified account. If it is not necessarily verified, then check to see if you can find the artist on other social media accounts. You can ask them directly if the artwork you buy is theirs, and even confirm their account.
- Dodgy Storage Sites, where NFTs have the ability to go missing once you have purchased them. This is where smart contracts get involved. Remember that the contract often is stored and in a different place than the artwork. So do not buy an NFT that has a set linked to a URL that leads to an image. This is because an artwork stored on that URL could be changed and removed without your permission at any time, and the token you hold basically holds a link...not that actual artwork or digital file you wanted to buy.

Common Cryptocurrency Scams

- You want to look out for the same or similar phishing scams.
- Watch out for fake celebrity endorsements, where sophisticated scammers can design brochures or fancy websites to show celebrity endorsements on phantom cryptocurrencies that do not really exist.

As a beginner in the cryptocurrency world, it is recommended for you to avoid ICO (Initial Coin Offerings). This is because this platform is riddled with too many risks and too many scams. Yes, customers are promised discounts on the coins they buy, but there are over 10,000 different coins out there, and thousands that are going to fail in the future. So do not take any blind or unnecessary risk as a beginner and stick with crypto coins that have already proved themselves over a certain period of time. This would be the crypto coins in the top twenty list, but specifically Bitcoin and Ethereum.

Your safety online should be your priority. So remind yourself to be careful every single time you login to the web. Do not take any unnecessary risks, and remember the online world is full of friendly faces on screen, but behind the screen and those typing on the keyboard are a very different story.

Chapter 9: Understanding How to Work on Exchanges and With Brokers

Okay, so if you are going to use stocks, you will need to learn how to work with brokers, and what to look out for them. If you want to use NFTs or cryptocurrencies, you will have to learn about exchange platforms and which ones you will want to use.

There are many exchanges available, and you should feel free to explore and find out which ones suit your fancy. But there is one very important aspect of the exchange you are always going to have to look out for:

- Security

Exchanges are a very common target for cybercrime and hackers. So you want to choose an exchange that prioritizes security above all else.

Exchanges Explained

What exactly are exchanges? They are platforms where people come together online to buy, trade, and sell different assets. There are exchanges for cryptocurrencies, for NFTs and for stocks.

Bitcoin is joining some of the official stock exchanges, but it is going to take a good long while before we see a merging between the different exchange platforms.

Here are some things you want to look out for in crypto exchange apps:

- Crypto selection, how many choices do you have? How many cryptocurrencies can you buy? What is the use of using an exchange platform if it doesn't even have the coin you want to work with?
- Security, as mentioned above, I will mention this again. You need good security when it comes to cryptocurrency exchange platforms and NFTs.
- Fees, now this gets a little more complicated, but normally in an exchange, you will be faced with commission costs, trading fees, and more. Be sure that you understand the fees that come with the trading platforms. However, do take note that the fees on NFTs will vary per transaction purely because of the fluctuations and the fact that you will be charged based on how much traffic and how busy that blockchain is at that point and time.
- Availability, if you can't access it in your country then there is no use in using it. Certain exchanges are not allowed or available in your state while others are. So take your time

learning about the platforms, and make sure you can actually work with it in your country. The last thing you want is a splitting headache and studying Binance for over five hours only to find out that it doesn't work in the US, but that Binance.US (they are from the same brand but different exchanges) does. So save yourself a lot of hair-tugging frustration and make sure it works within your country.

- You also want an exchange platform that is compatible with the wallet that you are using. It is a very convenient step, as well as a security measure. Because although a lot of platforms offer wallets, it is not altogether always recommended for you to use them.
- Some crypto platforms do offer you rewards for the holdings that you have, so that would be a bonus. And some accounts have been known to yield up to 10% on certain coins. However, do remember that these accounts are not insured by the FDIC which means if you lose your money, you are probably not getting it back.
- Customer service if anyone has suffered from companies it would be because of terrible customer service. If you are a beginner and you want to save yourself a whole lot of stress, then find yourself a platform that is both user-friendly and has moderate to good customer service ratings. Trust me, this will radically improve your experience.
- Certain platforms will allow you to use your debit card directly in the exchange platform. If

this is something you would like to do, then be sure to keep an eye out for this feature on different exchanges.

Top NFT Exchanges to Look At

- OpenSea
- Nifty Gateway
- Rarible
- Binance NFt
- SuperRare
- Async Art

Top Crypto Exchanges to Have a Peak At

- Coinbase
- Crypto.com
- Gemini
- BitMart
- Kraken
- Cash App
- Bisq

Brokers Explained

Or if you need to try your hand out at stocks or want to use a broker service for cryptocurrency, then that is also a possibility.

*Tip: if you intend to work with a lot of cryptocurrencies, then it is recommended for you to use a broker. If you intend to work with smaller amounts of money, then it is recommended for you to use an online exchange platform.

But when it comes to stocks, the majority of the time, you have to work through a broker. A broker is those who deal with the clients directly and companies. There are also broker resellers who act as intermediaries between the prominent broker and the clients.

However, it is better if you were to work with a regular broker. Now you can work with a full-service broker or a discount broker.

And this depends on your goals and your budget.

Discount brokers involve that you make all your decisions, and you are just going to be telling your broker on what trades to make. Certain discount brokers do offer some advice on a trade for a fee, but that is about it. As a new investor, it is recommended to go with a full-service broker. You will have to pay more, but they go out of their way to give you the best financial advice, build an investment plan, and give you a better service.

But realistically, you are probably working with a budget, and this might not be so doable.

And you will have to first consider a brokerage fee, and many of them require a minimum balance before you can set up an account. For online brokers, it can range between $500 - $1000.

You will also have to face the possibility of withdrawal fees.

So when you are choosing a broker, make sure you understand just how the fee-structures work, as well as the fine print. Most common fee-structures work per trade, where a broker charges you a percentage of the trade.

Other brokers have a more complex structure, and this is where you really have to be careful. Do not use a broker if you do not understand what or how much you will be paying. Many brokers are slippery like that, and it can work against your goals, especially if you have a limited budget.

Some online brokers offer zero-commission trading, but then they pay to be on the other side of your trade. This can be seen as a form of unfair practice and could result as a conflict of interest (having a broker bet against the customer), which may lead to a ban of this form of structure in the future.

Which One Should You Choose?

You want to make sure to vet your broker, that means your broker needs to have passed:

- Securities Industry Essential Exam (SEI)
- Or the SEries 7 General Securities Representative Qualification Exam if they entered the profession in 2018
- Majority of brokers have also passed the Series 6 Investment Company/Variable Contracts Products Limited Representative Exam

*Tip: You can get this information on your broker by looking them up on: FINRA BrokerCheck

If you want to look for an alternative, you can consider using a robo-advisor, which is an automated trading and investing platform. They are a kit cheaper, and the investment funds won't eat into your budget.

But you won't have a lot of choices or personalization as Robo-advisors primarily set their sights on ETFs or mutual funds.

Chapter 10: Metaverse and NFTs

The metaverse is literally at our doorstep, and no, it's not just the Facebook or WhatsApp Meta that has appeared on our screens, as the metaverse extends to a digital world that is well beyond.

You have probably come across Mark Zuckerberg's virtual replica when Facebook had been rebranded Meta, as well as the live concerts that had occurred within the Fortnight Universe, and the word is now abuzz in the metaverse.

The Metaverse Explained

The metaverse is basically the 3D version of the internet. It is an immersive digital world which will revolve as a parallel for what you can do in the real world. For example, you can play games, explore museums, attend classes, and interact with people worldwide all in one platform.

It is not going to be just one big video game, although the gaming aspect is going to explode. Considering the gaming industry is already a billion-dollar industry, the gaming world is practically building the metaverse.

The rest of the world and functions are going to be catching up.

This is because there are certain games that already exist and work a lot like the metaverse. Although there is no singular gateway to access the metaverse at this point, you can enter platforms such as Decentreland, Horizon, Fortnight, Roblox, and Sandbox that all work a whole lot to enter the metaverse.

It is likely that for now, we will all be accessing the metaverse using our smartphones, tablets, or computers.

But in the future, it is likely to look a lot different.

And What About Crypto and NFT?

Well, the majority of the metaverse-like platforms are actually being built on Ethereum's blockchain. Let's start there. So Ethereum is highly likely to play a huge role in the future of the metaverse.

Secondly, NFTs can act like a digital form of possession of unique items and virtual land. NFTs are already being used in the games, and their design just makes sense that they will play a critical part in the metaverse.

And just like NFTs are going to play a role, cryptocurrency is going to be used to connect the real-world currencies to the digital one.

So although we are not quite there yet, you cannot deny the potential both crypto and NFT hold within the oncoming future. So, it would be wise to keep monitoring the metaverse, which blockchains are being used, and what people are considering using NFTs for.

However, you should also keep an eye out for the environmental impact of both crypto and NFTs. This is because the world is becoming a whole lot more aware of its need to change. So despite the great potential and technology of NFTs and crypto, if they both have too much of an impact on the environment, you may see the world turning quickly against it.

Conclusion

And now, you are at the end of this book, but this is far from the end of your journey. There is a lot that you can still learn about crypto, NFTs, and investing as a whole. The foundational knowledge has been set down, but as you start investing, you're going to have to dive even deeper.

However, with the foundations in place, and a general map, it should not be too complicated to travel through the different aspects of investing and can give you the necessary direction you need to take.

So, to summarize, you have learned all about the aspects of cryptocurrency, the pros and risks, and how blockchain works.

You have also discovered how NFTs work, how you can make money, and the fact that you need to approach it with more entrepreneurial aspects. You will have to build yourself an online community in order to build values on your own NFTs. If you want to buy and invest in NFTs, then you will have to learn how to identify the different potential of NFTs and learn which ones you should buy and sell.

You have also learned about stocks, the pros and cons of investing in stocks, and why you should consider investing in all three in order to diversify the portfolio that you have and reduce the risks.

We have also covered exchanges and platforms, and how to work with brokers, considering that if you want to invest in stocks, you will have to work with a broker.

And at the end of the day, the best thing you can do for yourself is take your time learning. It's not an easy journey, but it doesn't have to be so hard either. NFT, crypto, and stocks are really over complicated in many of the different articles, but it is available for everyone. In fact, people are more likely to have better access to cryptocurrency because they have access to WIFI than to proper banking services.

The world is still changing and evolving. You will need to keep an eye out for what regulations are put in place, but you cannot deny the potential that rests in working with these decentralized finances.

It is all so exciting!

Glossary

Analysis: the method of studying something
Assets: items of resources owned by a business, government, or person
Bitcoin: the original cryptocurrency designed by Satoshi Nakamoto
Blockchain: digital ledger
Chart: a sheet of information
Cons: disadvantages
Corporate Sector: the section of business
Cryptocurrency: a form of digital currency
DCA: Dollar Costing Average: popular trading strategy
Digital Currency: form of virtual money
Diversification: technique used to reduce risks by spreading investments
ETFs: Exchange-traded fund, a pool of securities you buy through a brokerage
Ethereum: second-largest cryptocurrency in the market
Exchange platform: platform used to exchange certain assets
FOMO: Fear of Missing Out
Gurus: advisor or mentor
Inflation: the substantial rise of prices in general
Investing: to put money into an asset with hopes of receiving a greater return
Japanese Candlestick: representation of time on a chart

Volatility: tendency to make changes in an unpredictable way
Ledger: record of transactions
Liquidity: the ability to convert something into cash
Loans: the act of lending or temporary use of something
Mining: the act of verifying and confirming data on the blockchain through use of Pow or Pos
Mutual Funds: a company that adds all the funds together from investors
NFT: non-fungible token, a token that is irreplaceable
Pros: advantages
Savvy: experienced, well-informed
Scalability: the ability to adapt something to increase the demands
SEO: Search Engine Optimization
Trading Psychology: the emotion or mental state that occurs during trading success and failures
Trading: the process of selling, buying, and exchanging different commodities
Trends: a general course

References

Artzberger, W. (2022). *Avoid these 8 common investing mistakes.* Investopedia. https://www.investopedia.com/articles/stocks/07/beat_the_mistakes.asp

Brunnhofer, L. (2022). *Best NFT tools.* Weirdo.rocks. https://www.weirdo.rocks/reviews/best-nft-tools

Central Bank. (n.d.). *Seven tips to avoid online fraud.* https://www.centralbank.net/personal/security/security-news/seven-tips-to-avoid-online-fraud/

Chianis, A. (2020, September 8). *Common internet scams & how to avoid them.* SafeWise. https://www.safewise.com/blog/internet-safety-avoid-online-scams/

CUInsight. (n.d.). *10 tactics scammers use - First Community Credit Union.* First Community. Retrieved May 2, 2022, from https://fccu.org/blog/2020/07/10-tactics-scammers-use

DeMatteo, M. (2022, January 18). *NFT scams: How to avoid falling victim.* Coindesk.

https://www.coindesk.com/learn/nft-scams-how-to-avoid-falling-victim/

Euromoney Learning. (2022). *Blockchain explained: What is blockchain?* Euromoney.com. https://www.euromoney.com/learning/blockchain-explained/what-is-blockchain#:~:text=Blockchain%20is%20a%20system%20of,computer%20systems%20on%20the%20blockchain

FCA InvestSmart. (2021, October 4). *Understanding high-risk investments.* FCA. https://www.fca.org.uk/investsmart/understanding-high-risk-investments

FINRA. (n.d.). *The reality of investment risk.* https://www.finra.org/investors/learn-to-invest/key-investing-concepts/reality-investment-risk#:~:text=When%20it%20comes%20to%20risk

Hong, E. (2022). *How does Bitcoin mining work?* Investopedia. https://www.investopedia.com/tech/how-does-bitcoin-mining-work/#:~:text=%22Mining%22%20is%20perf ormed%20using%20sophisticated,costly%2C%20and%20only%20sporadically%20rewarding.

Investopedia Team. (2022). *Top 7 technical analysis tools.* https://www.investopedia.com/top-7-technical-analysis-tools-4773275

Joshi, S. (2022, March 15). *The Metaverse, explained for people who still don't get it.* Vice. https://www.vice.com/en/article/93bmyv/what-is-the-metaverse-internet-technology-vr

Kaspersky. (2021, January 13). *4 common cryptocurrency scams and how to avoid them.* https://www.kaspersky.com/resource-center/definitions/cryptocurrency-scams

Picardo, E. (2021, April 30). *Investing definition.* Investopedia. https://www.investopedia.com/terms/i/investing.asp#:~:text=Investing%20is%20the%20act%20of

Software Testing Help. (2022, April 15). *19 best crypto portfolio tracker apps [2022 RANKING].* https://www.softwaretestinghelp.com/crypto-portfolio-tracker-apps/

Trends 0, S. H. I. T. (2022, March 1). *8 NFT scams to avoid.* Small Business Trends.

https://smallbiztrends.com/2022/03/nft-scams.html

Zeen. (2022a, February 25). *Best crypto paper trading apps & simulators*. https://zeen.com/best-crypto-paper-trading-apps-simulators/

www.ingramcontent.com/pod-product-compliance
Ingram Content Group UK Ltd.
Pitfield, Milton Keynes, MK11 3LW, UK
UKHW011020310726
14089UKWH00002B/6

9 781957 945071